Pre-reader

All About Bears

Jennifer Szymanski

NATIONAL
GEOGRAPHIC

Washington, D.C.

Vocabulary Tree

ANIMALS

BEARS

WHAT THEY HAVE

fur
nose
teeth
paws
claws

WHAT THEY DO

hide
sniff
eat
catch
walk
swim
dig
climb

Asiatic black bear

There are many
kinds of bears.

All bears have fur.
Some bears have black fur.

black bear

brown bear

Some bears
have brown fur.

Polar bears have fur that looks white.

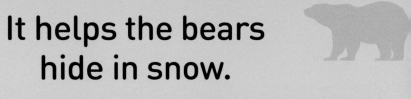

It helps the bears hide in snow.

polar bears

brown bear

Bears use their noses
to find food.

honeycomb

This bear sniffs
for honey. Yum!

Bears eat a lot of different things.

black bear

Some black bears have brown fur!

This bear eats fruit.
It also eats bugs and eggs. 11

A brown bear can catch fish with its teeth.

brown bear

sun bear

Sun bears love
to eat coconuts.

giant pandas

Giant pandas munch bamboo stems and leaves.

paw

They hold the stems
in their special paws.

Bears also use their paws to walk. They walk on four paws.

Andean bear

polar bear

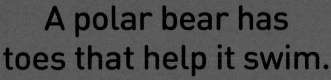

A polar bear has
toes that help it swim.

A sloth bear has very long claws.

sloth bear

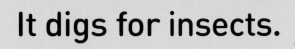

It digs for insects.

A bear cub uses its paws to climb.

brown bears

And to hold on tight!

Kinds of Bears

There are eight kinds of bears in the world ... and in this book! Here is what they are called.

ASIATIC BLACK BEAR

BLACK BEAR

BROWN BEAR

POLAR BEAR

SUN BEAR

GIANT PANDA

ANDEAN BEAR

SLOTH BEAR

YOUR TURN!

Tell a story about a bear.
What does it look like? What does it do?

eat

swim

dig

climb

To Betsy, because ... bears. —J.S.

Author's note: The bear on the title page is a sloth bear. The bear on this page is a sun bear. The bear on the cover is a black bear.

The author and publisher gratefully acknowledge the expert content review of this book by Dr. Rae Wynn-Grant, Large Carnivore Ecologist and Last Wild Places Initiative Fellow for the National Geographic Society, and the literacy review of this book by Kimberly Gillow, Principal, Chelsea School District, Michigan.

Published by National Geographic Partners, LLC, Washington, DC 20036.

Designed by Anne LeongSon

Photo Credits
Cover, Doug Lindstrand/Designpics/Adobe Stock; 1, Sylvain Cordier/Biosphoto/Alamy Stock Photo; 2-3, IsadaMW/Shutterstock; 4, Ghost Bear/Shutterstock; 5, Erik Mandre/Shutterstock; 6-7, Norbert Rosing/National Geographic Image Collection; 8-9, Rob Christiaans/Shutterstock; 9 (INSET), Subbotina Anna/Adobe Stock; 10, Ron Erwin/Alamy Stock Photo; 11, Danita Delimont/Getty Images; 12, Andy Rouse/Getty Images; 13, Daniel Heuclin/Biosphoto; 14-15, Chris Wallace/Alamy Stock Photo; 15 (INSET), clkraus/Shutterstock; 16, Philippe Henry/Getty Images; 17, vlad_g/Adobe Stock; 18-19, photocech/Adobe Stock; 20, Dmitriy Kostylev/Shutterstock; 21, Erik Mandre/Shutterstock; 22 (UP LE), Eric Baccega/Minden Pictures; 22 (UP CTR), Menno Schaefer/Shutterstock; 22 (UP RT), USO/Getty Images; 22 (CTR LE), Thomas D. Mangelsen/Images of Nature Stock; 22 (CTR CTR), MollyNZ/Getty Images; 22 (CTR RT), Royalty-Free/Corbis; 22 (LO LE), C. Huetter/Arco Images/Alamy Stock Photo; 22 (LO RT), Nimit Virdi/Getty Images; 23 (UP LE), Bryan Faust/Shutterstock; 23 (UP RT), GTW/Getty Images; 23 (LO LE), photocech/Adobe Stock; 23 (LO RT), Erik Mandre/Shutterstock; 24, Yatra/Shutterstock

Trade paperback ISBN: 978-1-4263-3484-9
Reinforced library binding ISBN: 978-1-4263-3485-6

Printed in the United States of America
23/WOR/4